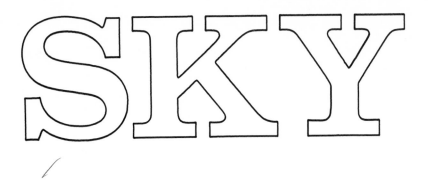

SKY

By MICHAEL BENEDIKT

Wesleyan University Press

MIDDLETOWN, CONNECTICUT

Many of these poems have previously appeared in periodicals. For permission to reprint and for copyright assignments, grateful acknowledgment is made to the editors and publishers of *Ambit, Bennington Review, Chelsea, kayak, Kenyon Review, London Magazine, Modern Poetry Studies, New American Review, Paris Review, The Seventies, Stand, Sumac,* and *The World.*

"Money," "On Earth," "Psalm I," "Psalm II," "Psalm III," "Psalm IV," "The Sky," "The Statue Speaks," "Water," and "The Wonders of the Arm" first appeared in *Poetry.*

Acknowledgment is gratefully made to the John Simon Guggenheim Memorial Foundation for a Fellowship implementing completion of this work.

Hardbound: ISBN: 0-8195-2052-7
Paperback: ISBN: 0-8195-1052-1
Library of Congress Catalog Number: 75-120257
Manufactured in the United States of America
FIRST EDITION

NOTE: *These poems were written in 1967/8/9 and appear in approximately chronological order.*

Contents

III. A CHILD'S GARDEN OF VERSES

I. THE ENERGY CHEST

WATER

"You are very fond of water" — *My Horoscope*

The ear dips down and drops over the drips,
The clicking of a lobster claw
And the sound that shadows from the bottoms of boats make over the
    delicate dendrons of sensitive plants.
The ear of a drowned sailor speaks
From the deck of creaks
And a handful of change in the pocket of the *Titanic*'s Head Registrar
Fills the ear of the modern bursar
Cruising by, in the contemporary pleasure submarine, with a species
    of sprinkles.
Here, where the tides are still more silent
Here, in the teacup I am stirring
Even the crumbling of sugar makes avalanches
And the tea seething around the little spoon paddle is the sound of
    kayaks going downstream by degrees, bumping;
And here in the bathtub
I can hear the swishing of two feet that float
The lifting of little hairs from the ankle, and also the big hairs.
So I am here with my ear to the water
Listening for the secrets of the sea, again.
As long as living, which others today say is concentration,
Is discovered to be distribution, really,
We will love and listen to waters.

London, June 1968

COUNTRY LIVING

If all the finest perceptions in the world were to be dropped into the
    feet of a diving suit, or space suit
As sole weight
How we would laugh to see a gentleman in a diving suit floating
    outstretched upon the water, signaling for help; or a gentleman
    in a space suit with an astonished look, floating off at the end of
    a tether!
If all the keenest ideas were placed in a prescription bottle beside bad
    butter at a barbecue table
All the guests would go home anyway and hiccup

Everything is in its place, everything is now in its place

Still, to face the southwest and watch streetlights against sunsets
Or to observe star reflections in a dying aunt's lorgnette
Or the sea sucking in and out between two rocks
Or the feeling of sand in my sneakers
Is to listen, to think to hear
Little dialogues of spirit and matter

1.

The morning glory outside my window was planted so late in August
    that it only had one flower, and that came on October first, before
    the frost killed it;
We called it "Evening Tragedy"

2.

Dabbing at our eyes with our handkerchiefs we listened for the flow of
    tears running down our breasts
And recalled stories of how Great Oaks have sobbed when cars collide
    with them in Redwood Forest; how large liana vines have been
    frustrated en route to their destinations, interrupted by a small
    boy's foot
Of moss, that moans like Jews
Of jolly woodchoppers' axes that ring out in the morning, branches that
    squeak when the true sons and daughters of traditionalist poets (all
    those who think that they own the Earth) come to swing on them
Cries that emerge from petunia patches gone dry
Beanfields weeping in the sun in Spain, tales of undamp cotyledons
As well as the everlasting shrieks of weeds.
(I see their bodies stacked up in yards, preparatory to later burial
    or burning)

3.

Talk to a plant next time you see it and a plant will say something nice
    back to you
My wife was growing a snakeplant and a fern, but she loved the
    snakeplant most, and said Hi there to it every morning; so it put
    out a flower in return, lovely, even though it was of course ugly,
    waxy, hairy and funny-looking

My wife read a book that spoke of the sounds of protest from flowers
  uprooted, which have recently been registered in California
  on seismographs
So go — and whisper to roses

THE FUTURE

The future is withdrawn again.

Just as the donkey's teeth are pressing against the carrot, somebody
removes the donkey.

If this is all the future holds for our nation's donkeys we may never
make it through the forthcoming year!

What we need is a future in which vegetable gardens are planted in
the atmosphere.

Gnash gnash.

Each step of the way must be marked by a half-eaten tuber or legume
tossed aside, as if luxury were everyday

Or, as if donkeys could now go in any direction they wanted, even into
the past.

Advancing on all sides, listen to the delicate steppings and droppings
of the donkeys, catching up to the future, making the past come
alive sooner and sooner.

When the future is finally achieved, the valley of the world will see,
strewn as far as the eye can see, donkeys sitting down or lying
around at their ease, little carts unhitched and parked; we will be
aware as never before of the portability of time

CLEMENT ATTLEE

1.

Except for me, nobody remembers Clement Attlee.

The winds of change and cold snows, too, have flowed all over his
features and figure, and now all we can see is a Sherlock Holmes cap
and large pair of earmuffs.

Occasionally, a bear comes by and finds a boot to bite.

Oh, wake up Clement Attlee, another inch of time and not only will no
one admit to remembering you, but nobody will be able to be
found who has really ever heard of you!

Clement, Clement! — Hi ho, first post-war English Labourite and
somewhat socialist Prime Minister — hi ho, hoo-hoo.

2.

The other day, in the moviehouse (after all these years, *I* should say
"cinema"?) a hundred people chuckled when a French general
with large weights affixed to his eyelids said he had once been a
member of the "underground resistance."

Upstairs, twelve students from nursery school are discussing the
New Order.

At a party, I finally meet God. He is with a student. He grimaces
a lot, the student.

Elsewhere, a graduate of Sarah Lawrence College is entering a mosque.

Apocalypse!

3.

Outside the covers of the bed, place from which all creation is sent
forth, I feel a shiny bald head, a bristly walrus moustache, and
imagine that under the covers, I am wearing checquered knickers
and carrying a walking stick. Cautiously, a frayed black monocle
cord starts to make its way back across my cheek . . .

TUBEROSES

Tuberoses wound around my feet
Spears of green in ears
I am a multiple plantholder, a statue, here by a running stream.
Lilac fashions pervade
Among these damp shoes, which do not parade.
These hands which I give to you have green growing beneath the
     fingernails
And greeting me well
Is like taking a walk in the woods.
Here Little Red Riding Hood rushes out of an old cobbler's shack, her
     clothing ripped to shreds again, her bonnet thrown back, and
     over her arm a basket of buns.
The Three Little Pigs are building a city.
The "Musicians of Bremen" are present.

MONEY

Funny money. It giggles as it goes. Whenever we are about to spend
some, just as we reach into our pockets, it goes "Ho Ho!"

Inklings may come to us that it is attempting to soothe us at the
expense of the truth, for after all, even to money that giggles
there is an end

But we go along with its masquerade, since we want to do what makes
it happiest.

Yes! — we want bills of large and small denominations both to flutter
with laughter in our hands

We want dimples on the face of all currencies, coins to be smiling as
they are slipped into slots

Every vending machine to be regarded as a cornucopia of jokes and
mirth, mankind receiving a smile with every gumball, candy bar,
soft drink, seat cover, pocket comb, cigarette, foot vibration, etc.

Gaiety residing in change purses and pockets

Piggy banks should squeal to be broken

When we walk into a bank, we want to hear tittering from the
tellers' cages

Muffled chuckles from safe deposit vaults

High hilarity from the halls

And the whole littered with packets of newly minted bills and rolls
of pennies and silver throwing themselves around on the
floor, guffawing.

But see how the ungracious bank guards seem indifferent to our
ambition.

Ever they face the doors, front and rear, regular or revolving, with
guns at the ready

Ever the shopkeeper will throw his body without hilarity over the cash
     register as we enter, with our fame
And vending-machine franchisers are taking special care to affix locks
     tightly to their product, and its goods,
While stockbrokers chew on pencils eternally, with sad looks

Tears every night create the river of our true hope and faith
Upon which borne along gravely is the contemporary barque of utter
     financial solvency

THE BLOCKHOUSE

In the blockhouse at the far end of the field where the powerful new
    bomb was being tested
The reverberations of the damage we do just arrived;

See how the brilliant young scientist standing next to the panel of dials
    drops his cup of coffee
While the experienced old engineer is tilted, and falls within the broom
    closet
The pretty young typist in the corner who is staring at the framed
    photograph of her boyfriend feels her eyes disastrously deflected
    directly onto the page in her typewriter
And observe how the Fuller Brush Man who has just entered the
    blockhouse feels his goods in their attaché case ominously jiggle
Just as a trembling comes over the green spears of a plant that has been
    thriving there upon the radiator

Even the janitor swallows his gum
Even the uniformed guard drops his gun
Even the charlady lets the fuzz escape from her dustcloth, that
    impeccable and portable dump
And oh! I just noticed a mouse who happened to be watching all
    this from the mousehole doorsill with his five small mice and
    their mother
Run hysterically away, the seven pink mousetails vanishing

A family; I don't even have a family

THE ARTILLERY PORTRAIT

Each cannon when it fired
Shot out a little cannon

Or else the smoke took the shape of the kind of gun
From which it came;

Or else the smoke meant
The shooting of a gun of smoke.

Oh, if the eye could only see
Only other eyes,

And the voice could only smell
The smell of the dead.

"In the formal garden of my acquaintanceships several architects grow,
  A bookseller, a librarian, a publisher of pop songs, the owner of a
      leading art gallery, a sandhog, a muscleman, a fishmonger, and
      twenty Instructors of English, all in a row,
To mention only blooms I see today.
In the morning I stroll among them all to encourage an interest in
      further companionship, those being such whetters of this appetite!
And in the midday, they make my business meaningful
And in the evening, over cocktails, they refresh the spirit

"A few weeds crowd the edge of my paradise:
    Yes, the seducer of pubescent midgets
    Yes, the cracker of long jokes that make the face grow grey
    Yes, the universal weeper in the corner, in every Executive
        Washroom
    Yes, the habitual despiser of Jean-Luc Godard and Bob Dylan
    Yes, the stoned youth, if helplessly wordless, or boring
    Mr. Jones, secret collegiate fingerman for the F.B.I., whom hereby
        I expose and identify for all time
    And the inner policeman, who would arrest the pleasant prostitute
        and abuse the amiable child
    Not to mention Ugly Presidents

"But I do not stoop to pluck them out
  No, do not stoop to pick them out in restaurant, cab, bar, farm, field,
      stream, concert hall, auditorium, moviehouse, football stadium,
      school, ice-hockey arena, and office

"No, for I am running
  No, for I am coming

Having in mind my own home flower bed
My pretty private joy, which is a boundless tract,
The rosebush jungle of my Wife,
To where I am returning at once, forever, after two or three more
  stiff Martinis."

THE SEER

As it is developed in space, the little apartment is developed into time.
At its front door, a jingling key, two thousand thoughts.
Also several concepts, and a single Ideal.
Just inside the front door, two bottles lie, one empty and large, the
    other small, empty halfway, and containing white pills.
Further on, a single vinyl boot.
Still further on, a plastic dress. Also a man's jacket, and a telephone
    kicked off the hook. A space, a space filled with darkness.
Doorway to another room. Two shoes. Dark inside.
An oval of light. Light, in lines, through the bamboo blinds. An oval
    mirror. A madras lampshade. A paisley bedspread. A lit cigarette.
    Two eyes, and an art periodical.
Oho! Aha! — Here is where you have been hiding, backed up against
    the far wall and shrieking for help!

THE ENERGY CHEST

The energy chest
One keeps on dipping in

With the hand of one's head
And one's chest is seldom empty

It's lively.
Even at night when we sleep

We see it
Standing by the bedroom window

Looking out into the distant valley, just standing there
On tiptoe.

THIS MORNING I FOOLED A BUTTERFLY

It was not real, finding an unmarked envelope of old seeds left by
    dead Dad

It was not real, finding them acting as a place-marker in one of
    the armaments catalogues of the electronics industry for which
    he worked

It was not real, that there was a place left clear for planting among the
    weeds that had ensued in the six weeks since his decease

It was not real that these seeds sprouted

It was not real that that happened after three months, during which I
    could hardly find the time to return for a visit to the garden
    beside which my mother lived in a cottage

It was not real that they were not tended, but came anyway to maturity

It was not real that, as I sat there in the garden, an insect came (some
    damned dumb butterfly) and, proceeding straight to the spot, sat
    on the product of all this accident, the issue of so much deflection
    and misunderstanding

And sat there on the tangle of unknown yellow and blue flowers, and
    roses, for a full fifteen minutes, as if all this were real

THE STATUE SPEAKS
for Bob Dylan

In the middle of the summer, the butterfly alit on the nose of
    the statue.
It had to be removed with a stick
And the person who removed it with a stick
Eventually had to be removed, pried up by God.
I myself would have fed remains of the butterfly into the statue,
    placing it upon the ledge of the copper lips
And waited for the wind to blow it in.
    Good heavens what a taste
    A little like sugar, somewhat like kale;
    I seem to have stuck my tongue into the jar of eternity.

ON THE LAWN

Just lie back, keep on and lie back, and something is sure to form
Even during the past two hours, while reading, twenty clouds have
    probably come together to form a big camel
So, disharmonious pieces of all time are apt to fall together
To form a single contiguous carpet. Here it will be convenient to walk
    and run. In the winter slide, in the summer sit, preferably perhaps
    somewhat as if at a café.
None of the pieces needs much of a push.
One does not arrange them as one might arrange gunboat formations
    in a harbor
Or grapes in an arbor!
Overhead now:

          Is that a camel?
          An enormous white bee?
          An umbrella stand?
          A fan, with dark lashes and red lips at the lace edge,
             looking over?
          A storm?
          A foot, poised for the next step forever?

GO AWAY

Go away, go away, and as soon as you come back
Be something better.
For example a shell — one that has lain for days on the edge of a
    beach, overturned and sparkling, light captured on an edge,
An oak-leaf-like cluster of sunlight that filters through elm branches,
An earring bobbing, like a float at high tide, against the neck of
    somebody very sweet,
A weatherbeaten motheaten coverlet,
Or the arrows on the arm of a diving suit or a space suit indicating
    where to thrust through the arms.
Think: in reference to the mainstream of human desires and wishes
What would you know now, if you briefly waved goodbye to the world?

II. EVENTS AND ENVIRONMENTS

COMING AND GOING

I. Passing Through Troy

Get the children of America out of Troy, New York! The awnings hang
    slackly from the door frames in that city
And sooner than usual every young sweetie feels the skin wrinkle
And soft eyes grow smudged as glass on the Town Hall clock.
As for the young gentlemen of Troy
All they do is sit on curbstones and spit on Greyhound busses, like
    those I am riding on, back to New York City
O cities of the universe
You are not improving anybody much
Except maybe, in some few of you, in the sections that are ritziest
And what child of twenty can afford to live in them except until he is
    twenty; and then after forty
Fifth Avenue I love you, but when will I live on you again? Seven
    more years must be waited;
By the time I can cross 67th Street once more, and again enter the
    Central Park Zoo conveniently
No doubt my favorite raccoon will be dead

In the playgrounds of Troy, New York
They have no monkey bars, but all these Lincoln Logs in cast iron
When they grow a forest in Troy, New York, it isn't cultivated,
    it's invented
Each leaf is a tiny tin can or a small nail file
The City Fathers probably think that the arrangement of gas tanks,
    barbed-wire-topped fences and offensive oildrums that surround
    the town, and constitute the suburb through which we are
    now passing

Is some kind of an arboretum.
That's just about enough about you now, Troy, New York

O children of the universe (who live in Troy, New York)
The mind moves on
We have just scratched the surface of the problem
And soon I will be out of the suburbs, even, of Troy, New York

But children of the universe (and of Troy, New York)
I make this suggestion: that the ugliness of Troy, New York, may be
    transcended
Move out
But move out to schools and communities in the country along
      the East Coast for example and become architects in more
      beautiful surroundings
Then come back, and for all people
Build more ritzy districts

So that the mind of man may hum with unearthly earthly beauty,
    which is only the beauty of materials
May you begin with the specific:
The maintenance of cities we can stand to stay in,
All the way from Troy, New York, to places in Georgia, like Athens

II. The Student of Wonder

   1.
There is a book in the head whose pages are constantly rustling
When the lamp of solitude is lit we read it by the light of silence
Bending over our head, with one finger following the lines, the way
    a roué or rapist will follow a lonely night-walking woman down
    94th Street, realm of the "residence hotel"
Follow her, until she begins to run

Her feet tapping down the sidewalk and through the halls of all these
   neglected West Side apartment houses, all sad domains
   without doormen
And wisdom is achieved, and proclaimed with a stifled cry

2.
Meanwhile, the other finger lies on the other side of the head. As
   if stuck to it.
It does not move but points perpetually
Indicating to the vital rays that are pressing in from without,
   and space, and the vibrations that are filling the room from
   the Great Nebula in Andromeda
The location of the brain, so that it may be enlightened, after several
   more decades of this.
Late, late, the student of wonder sits at the tables of thought, and
   in the chairs of memory, smoking the cigarettes of eternity

THE AUDIENCE FOR ETERNITY

The ladies all wear spectacular hats. But that's all.
The men don't mind; those who can't see over them can see
through them.
For eternity, the men wear burnooses and bowler hats, and carry
walking sticks as they sit. Also, they smoke stone cigars.
Every two months, they chuckle.
On stage, a blaze.
An entertainment:
Somebody installed a large mirror.

EVENTS

I keep on gesturing to the general, broadly hinting, but the specific
    keeps upraising its head
From out of the vast fields of the temporary the permanent keeps
    cropping up
Even atoms, which are famous for being full of surprises
Sometimes sit around or just lie there, when examined
So hello there I say to phenomena
So hi there they answer back
And we both know that this might go on forever and will

Yet already I have spent too long a time trusting the expectedness of
    events
At approximately 9:55 every morning I start off the coffee, creamless
    though I often may be
Knowing that the friendly milkman delivering will always stop by
    and tip his cap
And he does come, and under his cap he keeps his pet hamster OSWALDO
And the supper that I plan at 11 P.M., the intimate tête-a-tête with
    somebody very sweet
Is invaded by the hordes of Attila the Hun, screaming

But of course, other things than dinners matter
Other apt examples come to mind
Only I can't remember any
Knocking at the doors of unconsciousness
Experience will eventually educate the unexperienced traveler
Yet of all the days of my being, of all the days so far of all your being

All I recall is one small quiveringly sensitive white whisker from the
    pink-tinged blue muzzle of OSWALDO

ENVIRONMENTS

Environments, we admit you exist. Yet we refuse to pronounce this
    acknowledgment as if it were some kind of an affirmation
Dancing around the celebrated maypole of the walls, the ceiling, and
    the floor
I will not shake hands with the keys of my typewriter
Nor discuss things with the filing cabinet of this cubicle, or speak with
    the ungenerous and ironical syllables of a former poetic
    "eloquence"
And as for the section of sky visible at the window, this Real Estate too
    will not be the object of the joyous sparkling of any eye of mine

No, for now we will turn
Turn from the prevailing sounds of radios and TV's playing too loud,
    sounds of traffic screeching to a halt, sounds of brakes being
    applied (but when will brakes be applied to the mean mouth and
    its angry ideas? to bitterly tin ears?)
Turning from the various smells, touches, and words, the most
    comforting even
Leaving behind Professor Schlossberg's Need to Communicate
Revolving my senses finally
Until this eyelid is looking at this eye

That is why the boundaries of the skin are always throbbing
    and pounding.
It is assaulted by The United Forces, you know who they are (and I
    know who *you* are)
Feel for the last time circumstances, and their sincere and evil envy of
    anyone's secure cheer
I have just thrown my most precious possessions into your suitcase,
    thereby creating a vacuum

I will move house and life, now,
Transforming space and bearing time along,
Transferring all that there is to whatever will come to be

From around the corner of space, where walls have been completely
    covered by the grafitti of the aggrieved
Comes the incessant sound that seems suddenly to bear more of a
    relationship to the melody of a vigorous flogging, or some other
    contemporary massacre,
Than it does to the melody of flowers being dipped in and out of
    cool pools of water for a sudden if unconventional freshening.
Perhaps each mark on the victim's shoulder, in case one is left by now,
        is the same size and shape as the blue bud of the sweet alyssum?
Or the green tongue of the snake?
Or hell's red eye.
Too much color too much color!
Space will have to be wrung out now
Space will have to be dried all day
And all night, too, all night by the night watchmen of space, grumbling
    and retired, who take charge of things while we and they are
    asleep, those who punch the time clock, and then the space clock
The dream recalled in the morning will have to be without color (after
    you have wrung out space, throw away the rainbow)
Black and white also must go
The neighborhood of the universe must be divided up now into the
    idiots and the ones with the thoughts.
The refugees are lining up again,
With the burden of wisdom,
At the terminal of the visible

TIME MAKES MONUMENTS OUT OF EVENTS
after Robert Morris, sculptor and dancer

Time makes monuments out of events
Piling up the number of times you bit your lip, stubbed your toe, or
    hit your finger with a hammer
With the time two aunts were lost in a speeding vehicle, by virtue of
    a cliff
And several passable witticisms you made at a party in 1967.
Also, it reaches into its bag
To find the way you felt coming out in the central street in Pittsburgh
    after delivering a lecture on "Art in America"
The summer months spent at a high school in Jamaica, Long Island,
    where all went for special tutoring, who were relatively dumb
    in Algebra II
And the dissatisfaction felt with regard to certain ancient collegiate
    English instructors, whose idea of good literature so obviously
    meant bad art; and the memorizing of the rules of French
    grammar, while translating Mallarmé "on the side,"
Even the opening of this poem, with its first line so obviously "eloquent"

Sometimes, time pulls its arm out of its bag
And extracts a set of plans:
Someone's original scheme for your monument, geometrical, gleaming,
    white, and serene;
Time weeps then

VERTICAL CONSIDERATIONS

If you stand there too close, things that run past will run past ripping
off parts of your costume and body *en passant*
But if you stand too far back, you may prove to be like the person at
the edge of the Grand Canyon cliff being photographed by his wife,
who steps back to improve the focus but who ends up improving
the entire view, by falling off
But these are horizontal considerations.
Seven or eight vertical considerations:

(1) How to become God
(2) How to sharply reduce the number of mosquitoes which keep
on annoying the weekend guests at barbecues
(3) How to afford the rent for an apartment in New York City
which will at the same time be high enough to permit the
minimum daily amount of light and air necessary for human
survival yet low enough to prevent things accidentally falling
out of the window from breaking
(4) How high to raise the American flag
(5) How long to delay a trip to Great Britain until a reservation
becomes available on B.O.A.C., so as to be sure to receive
the benefit of beholding the charming British stewardesses in
their mini-blouses and maxi-bosoms
(6) Does a partial erection while running with luggage count
favorably in the sight of God?
(7) How to become an angel
(8) How to become a cloud

VERTICAL VIRTUES

After thinking it over, I think I definitely approve of things that are
    standing upright over things that are not, or that are lying down
Approve of the Eskimo igloo over the hogan
Of the watertower over the lake
The planets over the skies
Not to mention "I" over "U"
Over "U" which curves so insidiously from the right angular
If "I" were to be written "⊢" that might be different
But fortunately "I" isn't spelled "⊢"
And it is clear that "I" is the only sensibility for me
"I" shaped so like the beams of constructions,
The forms of the future building

THE BED BEYOND THE BED

There is a bed beyond the bed
When you are really tired
So that if you want to lie down
And think you have no place to go,
You do. For me,
It appears at any time
From 3 A.M. to 11 A.M.
Especially after doing something exceptionally pleasant
Especially after times when waking seems like dreaming
It turns night into day and day into night and the reverse
It appears after sex but there is no sex there is what I am trying
    to tell you
It's a conceptual bed you might say
With no possibility of conceiving.
You might say that you love it here
And that you can't conceive of such an other thing.
Look! In bewilderment you just blinked your eyes
And threw the covers all the way back
You just turned your head and when it moved
The pillows were plumped up invitingly.
You smiled: the blankets created hospital corners.
No it is not your body I want
When I get into the bed beyond the bed
No it is not that my dear not so much that any more
It is just having the chance to think
Of the bed beyond the bed beyond the bed.
There neither mind nor body need exercise or stir
Eternal isometrics go on
Love for all things
Love for all time

1.

Everything is coming down, except that whenever something drops
It meets something on the way up, rising,
So that the air resembles two-way streets whose sidewalks have
    converged and pedestrians been mingled
Hello, hello, say the shoes to the eye
Hello says the short insect's lower nether foot to the rainbow arc
Hi there says the hog swill flung from the pail at the back door;
Greetings answers my edition of Plato, from the windowsill,
Also I believe I hear greetings being exchanged at this very moment
    between the highest human accomplishments of all time and the
    37 cents the 42nd Street businessman actually ended up by
    swindling from me after 45 minutes of hassles,
And even between the writings so many of us, including me, once
    executed free for *The Village Voice,* earnest newspaper consisting
    about 75% of paid advertisements,
And the famous corporations who supported the 1968 "Festival of the
    Avant-Garde" (organized by Charlotte Moorman) for reasons
    unclear, but in a relationship which the same thriving
    "underground," "liberal" periodical says it finds "suspicious"

2.

There is a theatre opened up in Midtown or in my mind, unadvertised,
    secret and sacred
"The Little Theatre Just Off Michael Benedikt's Head," it is called
And on stage those ever popular favorites are entering, the lady saints,
    in long white robes
Then they throw these long white robes aside to reveal bikinis,
    perforated well, by Rudi Gernreich

And they stride slowly and gracefully all over the stage only pausing
    occasionally to bump and to grind,
Dance St. Theresa St. Barbara St. Anne and St. Charlotte
Not to mention the rest of you whose names I have forgotten, or
    which I never knew
Dance — or else if you can't dance, just jump about a bit, jump up
    and down,
For the horns of prophets are being raised, entirely electric
For the conch shells of shamans are replaced
With chords in sequences mostly parallel to C, E, and G
And the featured attraction is the Angel of Consciousness
Bust 42″, hips 44″, waist 28″

ON EARTH

On earth, everything is being improvised again;
Nothing was there until we thought of it
The flowers of reality bloom when we pour over them the waters
    of our dreams
Growing from deserts of our own devising.
Give up give up the heroic camel
The necessary enemy, and the gypsy tragedy.
It is obligatory only
To take to the air

THE SKY

After all this experience, the sky must feel the vast potential weight
Some of the birds look lighter than usual but consider the seagull
    lying there now in a ditch at the water's edge, like an old rock
When the sky sees the flamingo en route it backs off in horror,
    especially at the clumsy ones
It will not even stay in the same room as the ostrich
While hummingbirds fall with a thud
And flies and mosquitoes descend and resemble the overtones of clashing
    cymbals on an oscilloscope

That is why the sky goes around dropping airliners all the time:
The sky is tired
It has looked at the Boeing 747 Jet on numerous occasions and said
    "Enough is enough, I can hardly go on any more — but of
    course I must"
This is to say that it is less like an apprentice serving maid innocently
    dropping dishes in a Bavarian Alp
Than it is like an ancient faithful servant with an annoyed look, shaking
    drops of piss from a pervert's favorite mackintosh

That is why I would like to present to this august gathering of all the
    dignified people on earth
A concrete proposal:
Everything must become lighter
All phenomena of flora and fauna
When I reach for my cigarette lighter, for example *(he reaches for his*
    cigarette lighter, lying on the podium)
I want it to fly away before my hand, since my body has created a
    breeze *(the cigarette lighter ascends)*
When I am wearing the best clothing money can buy *(he parts his*
    jacket to exhibit his matching tweed vest)

I want it to be delicate as the web of the spider, the only creature
      which in the above circumstances is still able to fly, I might add
      in passing *(his body lights up, and we can see that he is wearing*
      a transparent vinyl jump suit)
When I am speaking the most profound thoughts, I want them to be
      both enchanting and thrilling *(he writes this poem)*
And when these ideas all age, I want to begin to disappear

FLICKER

The light of imagination is casting shadows in the corners of
    the drawers
Even those things which have receded from view for so long
Suddenly are illuminated; and their shapes, so bumpy, round, elongated
    and flat
Come to the inner eye.
But the inner eye is the same as the outer eye
The outer eye too has received the benefits of Light
If you could tell the difference between the inner eye and the outer eye
    you would have the right to receive some kind of an Award

Long nights, over this subject, scholars have pored
Bending down raptly over the human head, each starting with his own,
Besides trying to look for the inner eye, scholars for a long time have
    attempted to press reality right on the mind, directly
I visited a wise man in his apartment the other day and I interrupted
    him while he was pressing a big Biedermeier settee to his
    forehead; then came a potted palm, with drooping leaves, long
    and flaunting
Then he lifted the other remaining objects in the room, ending with
    ashtrays. Then he lifted me. It was certainly a short visit,
Yet I left that house that night with a light step, for I felt afresh
    to have been seen, definitively *seen,*
But since then I have changed my mind about his mind
And notice that this evening, while pouring myself my midnight cup
    of rum, I have disappeared

FATE IN INCOGNITO

At last I can figure out the nature of that whisking sound which I hear
    whenever I leave the room
It is not really the sound of wind through television aerials, safety
    screens, and the holes in old socks and underwear dangling
    on clotheslines
But Fate, rubbing its hands.
Whisk whisk it must certainly be wearing gloves
Whisk whisk or else it has fingerprints ridged and immortal as corduroy
And nevertheless, despite the threat
Here I am proceeding as if it were normal
As if a future came automatically, without one's having to predict it,
    without requiring that personal conception precede all
    circumstances and occurrences
As if any difficulties experienced last night, today, and tomorrow
And the tragedy of yesterday, with its latent triumphs,
Were not illusions of some will or other,
Harmony of hope and trepidation

"Whisk whisk whisk there you go again, Fate, swathed and
    whisking away
Now that I have thrown back your disguise and found you hidden
    under the mask of the whisk
I know, you will not go, and it is time for a new incognito"
(Listen to how clever it thinks it is outside our windows coming down
    the street again with that crunch crunch crunch squeak crunch
    crunch crunch)

III. A CHILD'S GARDEN OF VERSES

FOUR PSALMS
In Memory of Henry Rago, 1915–1969

PSALM I

Everybody has one thing about themselves. What thing? Whatever
    it is, there is only one of them. Everybody is running up a flag
    on which some Betsy Ross of the soul has embroidered a picture
    of himself or a graph of his brain waves with permanent pleats
To come out, it is necessary to select out all other things.
Nonetheless our atoms are entangled, our flesh is similar, also our joy
    and pain are the same, and this inclines me to gentleness.
Besides that, I carry the flag of the salamander, the leaf, and
    the newt
In my pocket, where the Polaroid photo my mother made of me
    used to be, I carry a picture of empty space, and of the
    water's edge

PSALM II

Nothing can be fitted into the past once it is over. No future act
    can be committed there, or inserted.
To be renewed, even the future has to wait around until more of the
    present arrives. This is also to say that nothing that will happen
    in the future can be made to have taken place previously
What is the present supposed to do during all this — sit around
    counting the grains of sand in an hourglass? Lie around playing
    Parcheesi? Indulge in games of chance?
Yes.
Past time is like a filled pyramid, while the future is like an
    apartment on Fifth Avenue in New York City, six rooms, at

$200 a month, with doorman; or one on Riverside Drive with
the same attractive features for $150; or one in the East
Village for $100. Or one on Canal Street for $50.
That is to say, both are impenetrable realms, only scarcely to
be imagined.
How was the world ruled before creation? How will it be ruled after
completion? At any rate, not by as pure a poetry as this

PSALM III

Everything is something. Everything that is taking place today has a
completely predictable fate:
Everything, eventually, is going to become History.
Even this meeting, even the very first time you read or hear this poem
Is going (in its small way) to become monumental
Gaining the grandeur that time sheds on events, its proportion, its
dimension, its particular light
This light is the definitive gleam on every circumstance,
The one that makes the lump a monument.
Even if the event seemed meaningless or boring
Hasn't it eventually begun to cast a shadow?
Everything is a big dark something that raises up its huge bulk from
the memorable New Jersey meadows, visible across the river.
With a vague sense of outrage and objection
All will swear, after leading any given life, that it has actually
been lived

PSALM IV

Nothing works. The gesture you made to say "go ahead boys, up and
at 'em" catches in the wind, carries you back to the beachhead

A valentine you sent to a lace-loving lady gets delivered to her dog,
who eats it, without reading it,
An octopus you ordered from the South Seas arrives without any arms;
and three weeks later, its little suction cups arrive in a separate
crate. You throw it out, thinking it represents all the buttons
you've lost from your shirts since the age of twelve. You imagine
someone has prankishly returned them to you just at the moment
when you've given up detailed clothing, switched to wearing
burnooses —
Nothing works. The mind is manufacturing infinite and irrelevant
amounts. The world awaits the invention of the conceptual wheel

ABSENCE OF ME

Ah! Ah! a great day a great life we are living too bad it doesn't
    happen to be mine
Mine is always taking place somewhere else at the time
Like the butterfly at which bad boys throw a brick
I develop a talent for absence and departure
So here I am on three sides in the War
Looking down out of the peephole of the bunker it is always me
    dancing the celebrated modern flamethrower torch-song "The
    Striptease of Flesh and Bone"
To see if I am really fond of you we lift you onto a tall stool so that
    your bare black bottom engarlanded with white lace lilies is
    silhouetted, assimilated, and assaulted; but whose inclination
    is it I create?
I am the whip and the victim, the dumbwaiter and the dinner
The letters I receive are all from me except for junk mail and various
    unsolicited advertisements.
I was the first one to think of everything that exists around here, in
    this poem
I live in this poem, it is my final, ideal one
Only perhaps my life is still going on elsewhere, perhaps it is still
    definitively someone else who is speaking

SITE

After 15 consecutive years of meditation, I finally figured out
    something of significance: the famous singing group
Bill Haley and The Comets
Was named after Halley's Comet, which was last seen in 1910
And which won't return to the earth again, and be seen, until 1986.
I have been dwelling on this subject, dwelling night and day, dwelling
    on it for so long that I am happy to announce that now, finally,
    I live there in it
It's a large, colorful country, a land of plains and endless perspectives
    ending in gesturing statues that shine and faintly smile in the sun;
    and in the foreground, there are houses with picket fences and
    window boxes with tabby cats sitting in the windows
Children run by rolling enormous hoops
And grandfather, adding stability to society as usual, is out behind the
    silo, dreaming of picking his nose . . .
Everybody else is not home, since they are all out being underpaid for
    their work. The Poet — the one with the wig and the quill pen
    sitting on the tall stool who tries to catch in a butterfly net the
    President's pretty daughter (the one with the long hair and
    bows) — the Poet is writing a page which will eventually
    undermine the state. He is engraving these words on stone; the
    stone is of a size that will slip under the Capitol building. He will
    pry up the President and overturn his Cabinet. What does the
    President keep in his Cabinet? His thoughts.
The other poet has simply left, enlarged and sticky, the page of a poem
    pasted like a poster on a wall, all over the world
It is nightfall and so meanings grow dark. Over the horizon the Comet
    rises, vibrating like a veil. This veil is either the veil that hides
    reality from us, or else the veil that hides the breasts of the
    first nude belly dancer ever to appear on television
Now, space is full of a low, murmuring singing
                 (reread first 4 lines of poem)

ADVICE TO ONE MORE NOVICE IN NEW YORK

Somebody is always looking at your body,
Remember that: even now, as you read this poem, somebody is spying
Trying to take note of the length of your waist, or to see up your dress
Nothing is ever pure.
Although a healthy, happy, not to mention obviously adjusted life
    requires abandonment of this particular perception, and the
    development of less sensuous forms of paranoia, palpable
    paranoia or political paranoia for example
Even inanimate objects are watching.
If I took you for a walk in the woodlands what would we end up doing?
    Dodging away from twigs and running from the looking of
    the leaves.
And as for the woodlands of Man
The subway is one big eye, upon whose eyelashes we ride, flickering.
In the bathtub, the hair is all damped down, and nothing is flickering.
There, the no-motion gives the feeling of you watching.
And of me, watching you watching.

LIQUID LINKS

1.

Insufficient as it is to me, my life affects others.
The anthologist out of Chicago telephones to his New York office;
    it happens to be at the same time that I telephone there from
    somewhere out on Long Island; and his secretary, when I request
    it, relays my regards
See how on my windowsill there are bottles containing vines I found
    broken off a mother plant. They turn toward the sun every
    morning but not without interest also toward my watering can and
    box of plant food
See how the thousand-year-old man gets out of the taxicab at the center
    of the sidewalk which happens to be the exact spot where I have
    been greeting visitors beneath a canopy wearing my doorman's
    cap and cape. Should I relinquish my grip on his hand, I realize
    he will topple to the curbstone, breaking into a thousand grains
    of old dry grey dust
A derelict smiles when he receives my dime.
Why is the entire universe one vast antenna
Awaiting my call, my touch?

2.

Beneath the lives of others, I notice my own life.
It is waiting there, beneath plants, animals, and objects.
It is waiting there beneath your underwear (hi there).
Just as the liquid links of our two bodies call to each other,
    signaling their chemical similarity
The liquid links of our two bodies call to each other.
We first began to notice each other beneath our eyelids, since it is
    always water there
And now, since your underwear is transparent, it is there where my
    interest is tending.

How does it feel to be 78% water? — Oh, sorry, I should know, I just
    forgot that I am 78% water as well.
Today I heard the liquid links of our bodies calling to each other,
    from valley to valley, from peak to peak, like mountaineers.
Here is what they said:
Hi ho, hoo-hoo, splish-splash, pish-pish.

LET ME OUT

Let me out! Let me out! I wasn't made to pour old onion soup down the
    toilet, I wasn't made to suffer from this dreadful cold
And the boy from the grocery store who is wearing this big cowboy hat
    and the fringed shirt and pedaling the bicycle with the big basket
    for food is saying, look! my soul is beautiful, too.
Oh William Wordsworth and the other 19th century poets from
    whose dear Romanticism I first drew hints
You have hinted me very well beyond myself
And now when I write poetry I don't know what I am saying any
    more, only what I'm doing
I even noticed that my loves weren't what they should be, thanks a lot,
    thanks a lot
Although surely all ladies with nice waists tiny tits and exquisite
    globèd asses shall continue to be superb
Let me out! I want to fly without having to stop at the airline terminals
I want to say farewell forever even to the departure points of La
    Guardia and Kennedy airports in New York
No, no, explicators; that doesn't mean I'd prefer to use Newark airport,
    after all dangerous Leroi Jones lives in Newark
Leroi, Leroi, do you want me to come to your neighborhood in
    Newark; if you don't, I won't
Leroi, do you remember the time you crashed that abominable
    cocktail party with your old friend, tall, enormous and powerful
    Charles Olson?
You both just entered, made three telephone calls (one long distance),
    and disappeared in one corner with the plate of hors d'oeuvres
    (Leroi, that must have been long ago, before the invention of
    soul food)
What is Leroi Jones doing in this poem anyway, is he making me
    immortal or am I making him immortal; certainly we are large
    this evening.

Tonight, after supper and an appropriate smoke, my cat started
  whispering to me, tales of the stockyards, and the sufferings
  she knows; for example the sufferings of beef on the hoof even
  as it is removed from the hoof for my supper, by blows on the brain
Oh big blows collapse us all now, it is our own heads we hit, our own
  arms
It is obvious all this, although it is obvious only temporarily
  during certain high moments certainly
And I agree with the recent revolutionary who said to me after our
  talk after our poetry reading: "It is in your poems alone that you
  speak prose for us"
But also with the host of the abominable cocktail party, whose fate it
  has been to be bitter forever
When will we see when will we really see we are the same and who
  was it anyway that the revolutionary meant when he referred to
  himself as me, and me, as "you"?
Who is speaking here anyway, can it possibly be me? — What is
  here and where is "I"?
And how will it be possible to fly with all this great weight of sadness
  and deliberation
Yes even United Airlines says we are five pounds overweight but as far
  as I'm concerned I'm 155 pounds overweight
I wonder how it would be to fly now I wonder what it would be like if
  love were really endlessly desirable possible and present
Let me out. Let me out! LET ME OUT!

ROSE

She makes herself a rose by standing around in your mind, growing,
She stands there on one leg and she says thorny things
But every time the sun comes she straightens up and jumps up almost
    another foot
A few more clear days and this rose will be through the roof
Passers-by in every direction will finally understand the secret
Of a love that far outran the pace of even the wonders of modern
    horticulture.
How many nights have you dreamt of such sweet cultivation?
Evenings of evil love, lying slyly with your arms around a vegetable
Swept off her feet, yet upset lest you see
A foot, like a root, fumbling down to real ground from between
    these human sheets.

THE ESTHETIC FALLACY

Here I'm madly rummaging around in the hall closet thinking it
    might be just the right way out in view of this fire at the door
And everybody thinks I'm a secret salesman of flashlights with an
    exceptionally fresh approach
Here I can't find the ladder, and am prone to fall into the fatal hole of
    all fire escapes
And somebody else tells me that he supposes that this is one more
    ingenious plan to advertise the need for plastic parachutes in
    the home
Oh Coleridge, when you wrote your *Dejection* ode, were you really
    sitting there next to your little opium pot covered in chuckles?
Baudelaire, did you actually take a series of sight-seeing tours around
    Paris to "get" new material
Is the patient who lies anesthetized on the operating table in
    T.S. Eliot's *The Love Song of J. Alfred Prufrock* really engaging
    in some new form of combined indoor and outdoor sport?
We have lingered too long in the house of many means and now our
    ends are desperately overdue for condemnation and/or urban
    renewal.
Send out the repair wagon, wrecking crew, and ambulance now;
Some flesh is real and ill

NAMING THE BABY

Everything is used up, everything is used up, everything is consumed
    by History.
Thirsty and hungry History, there is no such thing any more as the
    oasis of the baby
And we are prevented from starting anything anew or afresh.
Why else dear friends is it so difficult to name this baby today, to
    identify this human leaf of Eden, which we pray one day may
    arise, to join the tree of men
Why else are all children born wrinkled?

Byron will write many poems, then sink in the sea
Harrison is overly fond of tweed
Vladimir and Otto will compose electronic music
Jean-Luc will make movies
Oswald will shoot the president
Nikita's head is a knob
Rudolph has a red nose, or a concentration camp
Adolf will have an inscrutable fondness for Bavaria
Arthur enjoys round tables
Cedric will smother his uncle
Harvey thinks he's a rabbit
Felix will have a little high-pitched voice and show a marked
    preference for milk
Albert will promulgate the theory of relativity
While Phineas will purchase the circus
Estes will appear on television, heading a committee to investigate
    crime
Cliff will hurt his head by falling off some rocks
While Geronimo will also always be jumping off of or out of things with
    a cry
Phil will develop an excessive fondness for fried finches

Pablo will spend all day up in his room, thinking and painting
Rembrandt will always be borrowing money
You'll never catch Babe at home since he'll always be out in the lots
    with a bat and ball
Clark will fall in love with somebody named "Lois." A second
    possibility is starring in the movies.
Percy Bysshe will always strike some people as extreme
W.B. will write great verses which suffer initially from soft surfaces
W.H. will write great verses, suffering finally from hard surfaces
T.S. will write great verses but stop writing them too soon
Mick will wear tight trousers and walk around whispering
Donovan will dunk doughnuts and get drunk
Franklin will have a four-term Presidency, and then a cerebral
    hemorrhage
While Peter, Paul, and Mary will walk around all day
    eating immaculately conceived candy bars
Errol will always err
While Michael will accomplish much with regard to expanding our
    ideas of structure, despite criticism from the poetically stultified,
    dumb, and entrenched

No no don't ask me about possible names for this baby
All I can suggest is that we call him Time; for one thing is certain:
    surely Time must be born again

DEFINITIVE THINGS

No, no, they are never the same as their names
Nobody ever fits into his own definition
Who is it regards definitions definitively?
Least of all objects, yes, even those poor helpless things
Knife, you are a butterfly whose wings have been pinned
Pin, you are a knife whose butterfly has been removed
And the sky, which does not agree to stand up when somebody calls
    upon it
The sky, too, has its windows
See, then, how the word *window* grows troubled; it too closely
    resembles the word *widow,* and that's depressing
I have just said the word *alley* twenty times and find I have
    forgotten what it means: *alley, alley, alley, alley, alley, alley,*
    alley, alley, alley, alley, alley, alley, alley, alley, alley, alley,
    alley, alley, alley, alley — this blank look on our faces is actually
    a bright beginning
Next is next; I always forgot the meaning of the word *next,* even
    the first time I heard it
Madge, pass me the lung. The lung? That sounds too funny to depend
    on to breathe with! Other words are too short or too long.
    Pain seems too abbreviated while cling is almost always too short
And if *love* contains within it an appropriate little heart in its *v*
The problem with *death* is that it's too close to *breath*
Food equals fried only if you don't happen to be on a diet
Bundle, hunch, flaunt, corpse, lapse, kiss, fiddle, pelt, consume, erode,
    erotic, remake, tape, eyelash
Are 7 one-syllable words and 7 two-syllable words I like
I like all 3 and 4 syllable words for their more complex symmetry
Regarding the names of people, I would *like* to *refer* you to my *poem,*
    Naming the Baby, suffice it to say *here*
Like a hand that does not quite fit a glove
An eye and a contact lens, expectations and the world
Our definitions and meanings never quite overlap
Help help I'm falling off the edge of this page

MIRROR
(Poem-Event for Julian Beck)

I never thought I would start off a poem by saying "I sing"
But here I am nevertheless, about to "sing" something
I'm glad I finally decided to
The question now is what shall it be that I make a beginning by
    singing
Shall I sing about the pleasure of singing, would that
      be a waste of a song?
— No, since if I sing it, it starts to be so.
Since the song re-creates the singer, it is serious.
What I sing becomes irrefutable truth in the cornucopia of creation

In all song a really enterprising real estate agent should see lots
      where everything has yet to be established
Earth, rocks, grass and fences; expectations, dreams, and good wishes
      generally for everything
Yet I struggle all the time waste away the day half of what I do is
      contradiction
For example, here's a major theme: I find it barely possible to keep
      this right shirt cuff from protruding from my jacket further
      than the left. And there are other problems even, besides
So that I may say I am perpetually interested for all men in the details
      of improved relations between wrist and sleeve
My good wishes and embraces extend to you all with the same gesture

I know the joy of which we sing must be so,
Here, and in all other things,
And so I sing it

WAKING

Like a blonde queen who wears foam-white clothing, and who every
    night lets shining rhinestone panties slip down one leg, gliding
    through the darkness like a secret agent's shining Citroën
Like an arm outstretched for a palmful of Indian nuts at a party
The snow was falling.
Catherine the Great I remember you, images of your great lost
    grandeur penetrate my every waking dream.
Also, from last night, at the party, memories of some other Catherine
    I never knew

PRAYERS

Innocent days of illness and attending to oneself
Minor attentions, care, and daily devotions to the body
At whose shrine we regularly pray
Yet the mind looks on with a long, long face and a cross look
The spirit weeps tears like some kind of a lover bereft, or like
    some terrible mistress who hasn't yet received a present
It sits in the corner all during the long litany of Coricidin,
    Cheracol, and Vick's Vapo-Rub
Waiting for their Easter
When pleasure will be resurrected.
And you await me too, there at the edge of the field of lighter
    delights, tenderer doings, a love like a childish pastime,
    cherishing nothing
I await Easter the day of resurrection
And you, the Easter Bunny

ALL WOMEN ARE ONE WOMAN
For their Liberation and mine

All women are one woman congratulations on being such a particle
I can hardly wait to see the total woman what will she look like?
Perhaps she steps down from the mirror over my dresser perhaps she
    stands there streaming down rays and ideal solutions to
    present dilemmas
Perhaps even now she is stooping down to pick up a stogie from
    within one of the many great and famous Urinals of France
She could be something between these two; something like you.
Do you feel as if you might be part of something that is going on
    elsewhere at this very moment?
What part of the total woman do you think you might be, the erogenous
    zone, possibly? All parts of the body are Erogenous Zone.
I know without seeing all of you I knew it from only having seen
    some few of you, Woman
That when we abolish our boundaries when we cross the bloodstream
    of Man
Woman, woman, you will be the very first across

FOR JANE (AND ROGER) BUT CERTAINLY NOT FOR HENRY
or, *Barbarella*

Jane Fonda starring in *Barbarella* I have a message for you
I single out the Jane of *Barbarella* because there are other Janes
    and other movies, you have been cast and shot in many other ways,
    but it's this Jane of which I am fonder, Jane
How you appear in this film is no light matter, Jane
It appears that you appear nude most of the time, Jane
And everybody says it is the nudity in this film which is exciting
(Everybody that is except for the people who enjoy the weird
    science-fiction costumes you wear, and there are quite a few of
    them — I mean, there are quite a few of both weird costumes and
    people who feel you are remarkable because of them. For example,
    the three hip homosexual friends with whom I first went to see
    this film —
But that's unusual, let's just say that the majority enjoy the nudity.)
No, no, that's where they are wrong, like most public truth this is a
    truth which is too general, here there is a misapprehension to
    be corrected,
It is not *the* nudity which distinguishes this film, any more than it is
    the clothing which you threw aside that distinguished you.
After all, some day all clothing may go out of fashion, some day you
    may throw it aside entirely, there could come a time when nudity,
    too, could go out of style; it may become so ordinary that
    everybody will go around mistaking it for fashion; some day we
    may consider skin just one more maddeningly intimate form
    of underwear
So, just as it is your skin which justifies the clothing in this film
It is your body which justifies all nudity for me.
Jane, Jane, this is my message for you
Jane, Jane, this is my secret public message for you (and also for

your husband Roger Vadim, who happens to be the producer
of this film and who happened previously to be the husband
and director of Brigitte Bardot, whom I also didn't mind
too much)
Upon this crumpled paper written in invisible ink and doomed for
the outrageous oblivion of the audience for true poetry in the
present world of impossibly public perception we endure
I write that I too belong to this club of love, the secret society of your
most extraordinary and perfect bodily style,
Small bosom, large legs, narrow waist but exquisite hips and ass
that is larger than the ordinary, all located at a point not
greater than somewhere between 128 and 77 centimeters from
the floor

MODEST UNDRESSINGS

Modest undressings, not at all like the great ones of today's stage and
 screen, like that of Jane Fonda in *Barbarella,* for example,
You, too, may lay claim to the affections of sensitive men; I think of
 you, too:
Undressings in the doctor's office, innocent and indifferent, anxious,
 nervous undressings of schoolgirls in locker rooms outside
 gymnasiums, bored and tired undressings of people changing
 out of work clothes at the end of day
Solemn or hilarious undressings of nudists, or of people whose pants
 fall down by comic accident
Functional undressings for shower or bath, and the washing of
 corpses in mortuaries
And just as I do not forget undressings for ablutions, I do not forget
 sinkings in the sea like a diver, or sportings on the surface
 like a swimmer
Water is a great undresser; whenever I see water, I know that
 somewhere nearby someone or other is probably concealing
 himself or herself for undressing.
O do not forget the gentle undressings of the soft core pornography
 model! — sweet and soft — while the undressings of hard core
 are desperate and urgent
Nor do I overlook the activities of one who undresses for the sake of
 undressing, unprompted and unpaid, the tendencies of nudity
 within the context of art for art's sake, context of the true
 connoisseur of such modesty
Or the random undressings of true lovers, kept in secret like old leaves
 pressed between unreal pages, where only real fiends or extreme
 friends have pried;
Shy blossoms all fated to bloom as a blossom in the midst of some
 forgotten garden, to bloom and die deserted before being seen

by more than four pairs of eyes — or, as in the case of orgies, ten
or twenty pairs —
All still are flowers; though they may not be orchids, still, they are
surely no weeds.

TO PERSUADE A LADY
Carpe Diem

True, I have always been happy that all the things that are inside
    the body are inside the body and that all things outside the body,
    are out
I'm glad to find my lungs on the inside of my chest, for example; if
    they were outside, they'd keep getting in the way, those two
    great incipient angel wings; besides, it would be messy
I mean, how would it be if you reached out to shake someone's hand
    and there, in the palm, were a kidney and a liver complete
    with spleen?
Can you imagine standing at 5 P.M. in a crowded subway car full of
    empty stomachs?
What if a nearsighted old lady were knitting socks and suddenly her
    veins fell out? How would she avoid creating a substance full of
    strangeness and pain? To the barefoot country boy sitting on
    the edge of the bed in the morning opening Aunt Minnie's gift
    box, the sight of these socks would be what he'd call "a real
    eye-opener!"
And what if our voices touched? If our mouths went out, instead of in?
    If you were inside of me; or, at least, if I were inside of you?

AFTER A POETRY READING BY ALLAN KAPLAN

Allan Kaplan we are entering into an ideal arrangement between
    faithful brother poets
I steal a little of your style and you steal some of my subjects;
    following that, you steal a little of my style and I steal some of
    your subjects
Also, sometimes we look up from our work to discover that we both
    admire the same features on the same lady; her ass usually, it
    would indeed seem to appear
Ah if our eyes should meet they are full of applause for each others'
    judgment, an admiration in which a complimentary word here
    and there is nice, but obviously not necessary
So, here in this space, I would also like to comment specifically on my
    approval of two other aspects of your perfection which I noticed
    yesterday after your poetry reading: I mean your furniture and
    your clothing
And so we go through life, often abroad and not meeting for too long,
    but in reality perpetually like two celebrated wine connoisseurs
    who spend one weekend of perfect unforgettable drunken
    agreement closeted in one of the many pretty towers of Blois

THE WONDERS OF THE ARM

1.

This arm. It lies on the table like an old musical instrument or a
   dishmop, smoking a cigarette this time. I'm glad it is here but
   the question is, what shall I use it for?
It will express my will, or my whim, as words will; it's free
I say something or my arm does something.
There it goes again, traveling across this empty space again in order to
   pat the head of the lady who happens to be sitting next to me;
   or perhaps I risk linking arms with my dear friends, my leery
   familiars, the poets; my colleagues who do not yet know that they
   are comrades
Besides that, in the last five hours it has had a sufficiently varied
   schedule, writing a check, unzipping a dress, waving hello and
   goodbye, shaking the hand at the end of it, mixing drinks, lighting
   joints, and so forth,
Or admonishing the universe with uplifted Socratean finger.
Of course, sometimes it becomes my own admirer, I find myself
   patting myself on the back
Or shaking hands with my own hand, and agreeing to vote for it next
   November fourth. Fortunately, election day is November seventh

2.

Just think how efficient the arm is; imagine how it would be if
   whenever something had to be done by the hand of man, both
   arms always had to be moving and participating, simultaneously
   doing the same thing.
O the arm is very practical! It seldom engages in wasted motion.
The fact of the matter is, it usually ends up doing more than one
   thing with the same gesture.

For example, if I lift up a cigarette from this ashtray in front of me
   I am apt to tap off the ashes while doing so
When reaching across the desk to answer the telephone while it is
   ringing, the arm may pause on the way several times to neaten
   up objects scattered on the tabletop
If I turn the pages of any book, I may also use it to scratch the palm
   of the hand that is turning
Before, when I was patting your head, I might also have reached down
   with my long, playful and inquisitive index finger to tap you
   suddenly but gently on the nose.
But that's the arm for you, it loves experience, it loves and hates,
   laughs and cries at the same time, helps and hurts; one thing we
   must admit, it is not single-minded, you really can't say that the
   arm is half-assed.
Moreover: not only can the arm do two things at once, but sometimes
   each thing can have a double effect. For example, a Boy Scout arm
   may help a feeble old pensioner across the street, while in the
   meantime dreaming of seizing her legacy
But there it is again, that's the arm for you all over, incorrigible,
   indefatigable, and though it sometimes gets tired or changes its
   mind two or three times, it loves what it fears and hopes to
   overcome its fears, it likes life

3.
It is time to let your own arm wander now; let your dear arm depart,
   like inspiration's guiding star, like the muse's intermittent
   illumination, let it depart, hand spread wide, fingers and thumb
   outstretched, like the lark of lyric poetry
Let it touch everything and depart everywhere
Each finger being like a little ship, each finger a traveler with a little
   knapsack of nail on its back, loaded with blood vessels
   and sensitivity
And each thumb a tiny Columbus commanding
The four famous ships of his fleet, the *Niña,* the *Pinta,* the *Santa*

Maria and also the other famous ship which nobody but me
knows about and which sunk in the original harbor at Genoa.
Oh yes not only do I praise every single finger of the hand on the arm,
but also the thumb thereof
And some day we will compose other poems in this series, poems like
"The Wonders of the Waist," "The Joy of the Abdomen," "The
Miracle of Nostrils," "The Delights of the Leg," "Pleasure of the
Tibia and Fibula" or even a "Wisdom of the Human Forehead"
But for now, as you know, we do not trust the mind.
Let us compose our first new poems by sending them with fingers
outstretched, here and elsewhere, like explorers of the future, to
wander the keys of our typewriter
And so we will complete the body of our work.

SUNDAY MORNING: HYMN

All I want to know is, how come Jesus could walk on the water, and it's
    all I can do some mornings, such as those after a great party, to
    struggle to my feet and go out to the bathroom
I resist I protest I object
I am presently preparing a strongly worded note and wonder if I should
    consider breaking off diplomatic relations with the ineffable
Jesus Jesus when you danced on the Sea of Galilee, and made all the
    fishermen smile, were they smiling because they thought you might
    represent some new form of exotic catch
Were you worried about sinking too deep in the Sea of Galilee because
    it was rumored around Nazareth that Mary Magdalen had once
    peed in it?
Were you wearing earplugs against a possible descent; earmuffs
    against the first big blast of the singing of stereo angels?
Did your mother make you wear galoshes?
Oh Lord turn it down, turn down my memory this morning!
Ineffable, ineffable, all I can remember from the party last night
Is the medal of the nipple of a big black girl in a see-through blouse
I dream of a golden loving cup awarded in my mind to some passing
    blonde because I can well imagine her own personal golden
    loving cup
The heaviest hips act as paperweights for my thoughts
Too many asses too many tits
I am defined by my curiosity, checkbook, high school diploma,
    military discharges, skin and résumé
Ineffable ineffable I hear the lapping of little waves going faintly
    along the shore
I am here in the Middle East on the Dead Sea with my mistress and an
    expensive suntan; do the waves lapping along the shore make the
    sound of delicately capable little kisses proceeding up the slope of

a naked shoulder?
Ineffable ineffable here we go again we are out on the sand of a public
      beach doing our thing
Ineffable ineffable ineffable
Shall it be too late in the day of eternity before I finally truly arise?

THE WOMAN IN THE TREE

In the tree outside my window at 6 A.M., in a low voice, a dove
    is calling, Michael
She sings from far back in her throat, and shifts her tiny,
    brilliantly pink feet, which look like coral earrings
In another life I could have been her lover
Or maybe, if I raised the shade, and actually leaned forward from
    where my body is lying now, so as to look beyond my line of
    sight, where the dove is hiding between two twigs and singing
    in concealment from me
I will see a woman in that tree.
Now the singing in the tree swells, and becomes still more shrill,
And I seem to recognize her voice

REGRETS

I don't take too many days any more to do anything in
Almost everything must slip into the crevices of events
Squeezed between walls of intimacy, cheek by jowl.
My daily tasks bear about as much relation to "actually accomplished"
     as an automobile that has been squeezed into the wrecker's square,
     preparatory to strange Use, provisional upon the apparition,
     perhaps, of Rectangular Man
While all my future tasks are mere souvenirs of necessity

To and fro, to and fro the blood is rushing
The blood is traveling by Greyhound
The blood has just packed its bags with the usual complement of comb,
     toothbrush, magazine, extra set of spectacles, bourbon
     and phagocytes
But deep down in the capillaries
It wishes it could sit or lie down and rest, and think, as once

Oh friends, sweet leisurely beings with whom it was once meaningful
     to tarry
Here we are again in Tarrytown, New York
And the good and gentle times we spent return for a moment, with
     a cup of coffee half-sipped only in "Rose's Tarrytown
     Diner DeLuxe"
Rose is a big fat black lady who moves like clouds and who leans
     forward on the formica counter her huge arms to talk gaily
     with the face of the weary traveler who is en route
Oh friends, the times of our discussions return, good and gentle
Coming back from the times when our minds, too, had promise
Being Thoughts and not opinions and not the thing but the Symbol of
     the Thing
But all that is settled now

Things are what they are and there are so many of them that it is
all but impossible to pause
Beside your sixth cup of morning coffee, and the muffin plate with
eggs, I leave you my friends for hail and farewell for all time
this most affectionate dark rose